I hope you enjoy Nanas Hog—
Sue Miller

Nana's HOG

Written by
Larry Dane Brimner

Illustrated by
Susan Miller

Children's Press®
A Division of Grolier Publishing
New York London Hong Kong Sydney
Danbury, Connecticut

For Jan Cheripko, FFA
—L. D. B.

For my children, Alex and Emily
—S. M.

Reading Consultant
Linda Cornwell
Learning Resource Consultant
Indiana Department of Education

Visit Children's Press® on the Internet at:
http://publishing.grolier.com

Library of Congress Cataloging-in-Publication Data
Brimner, Larry Dane.
    Nana's hog / by Larry Dane Brimner ; illustrated by Susan Miller.
        p. cm. – (A rookie reader)
    Summary: Although people think her behavior improper, Nana rides a hog through town.
    ISBN 0-516-20755-5 (lib. bdg.) 0-516-26412-5 (pbk.)
    [1. Grandmothers–Fiction. 2. Pigs–Fiction. 3. Individuality–Fiction. 4. Stories in rhyme.]
I. Miller, Susan, ill. II. Title. III. Series.
PZ8.3.B77145Nan 1998
[E]–dc21   97-40045
                                                CIP
                                                AC

When my nana rides through town,

people stop.

4

PRETZELS

OPEN

They point.

They frown.

9

They don't think it's granny-like
to ride a hog through town.

They say, "Act your age."

"Use a cane."

16

"Try a three-wheel bike."

But Nana waves.

She rides on by,
her hog dressed up just right.

22

She shouts, "No thanks. Not now.
My hog's just fine.
Want to give him a try?"

They shake their heads.
They move away.

"That will be the day!"

My nana laughs.
She helps me up.

"Well—are you going our way?"

About the Author

Larry Dane Brimner writes on a wide range of topics, from picture book and middle-grade fiction to young adult nonfiction. He has written many Rookie Readers, including *Lightning Liz, Dinosaurs Dance, Aggie and Will,* and *What Good Is a Tree?* Mr. Brimner is also the author of *E-mail* and *The World Wide Web* for Children's Press and the award-winning *Merry Christmas, Old Armadillo* (Boyds Mills Press). He lives in the southwest region of the United States.

About the Illustrator

Susan Miller has been a freelance children's illustrator for more than ten years and has illustrated numerous books and materials for children. She works in her home studio in the rural Litchfield Hills of Connecticut, where she lives with her husband and two school-age children. They provide her endless opportunities for inspiration.